AF399353

Maarit Koivisto

Rose in the Heart

Poems

Finnish original Ruusu Sydämessä
published in Finland 2015

© 2018 Koivisto, Maarit
Picture on the cover: Maarit Koivisto
Translation: N.B.Bligh and Virpi Suomela
Publisher:
BoD - Books on Demand, Helsinki, Finland
Print:
BoD - Books on Demand, Norderstedt, Germany

ISBN: 978-951-568-427-1

To all roses and sparrows in everyone's heart.

1. A rose tree

In my heart grows a rose tree,
the branches illuminated by the sun of your love
with warm, golden light.
The rose in my heart is opening its buds,
the crystal water of love revives them.
Tweeting sparrow flies to the rose tree
and descends to its nest.
The rose in my heart and the tweeting sparrow
surrender to love.

2. The solar power

You are the energetic solar power,
that makes my flower open,
I surrender to your energy unconditionally,
I want to accept your light,
I open to your love.
I will love you with the light of my heart
and with the wisdom of my soul,
I strive to come to you,
we shall meet again somewhere,
You are like an angel to me,
all I want is good for you.
The rose of my heart blossoms only for you
spreading its mystical scent,
the light of my soul burns brightest to you,
you set all my torches on fire.

3. The tree of love

On the tree of love
blossom the amazing roses,
there can be nothing more beautiful,
than the sparkle in your eyes,
the roses of love spread their enchanting scent,
the infinity of stars open,
the ship of our love
sailing in the heady sea of roses,
the starry path twinkles in front of our eyes,
light years race by us lovers.

4. You

The sparkling stars of your eyes
make the sea of my heart flow,
moving in warmth,
to the beaches of infinity.
The happy glow of your smile
makes the flowers of my soul blossom
and the roses to scent.
My body moves with yours,
your heart is in my heart,
your soul is with my soul.

5. The waltz of love

I sailed with you with fill heart,
we danced the waltz of love,
when we danced, your heartbeat with mine.
The fire of your soul sparkled in your eyes,
the treasure is waiting,
to me your heart is the treasure.

6. The ship of my heart

On the helm of the ship of my heart
your hands are strong,
on the sea of life the course
towards the treasure of soul,
the sparkling diamond cross
may wait us behind the offing
when an island meets the eye.
The bright compass of nightly stars sparkles
its eternal light
when I trust the strength of your hands
and the definite steering.

7. The love in your soul

I read all beautiful in your eyes,
the story of love,
the story of life lived.
Your eyes are like love letters to me,
full of emotion, full of warmth.
In your arms I settle,
live pure tenderness,
give and receive the warmth of heart.
The love in your soul is a beacon to me
on the stormy sea
when emotions throw me
and the thoughts give no peace.
Your wise words guide me
safely ashore
and the home port.

8. The hall of love

I want to meet you,
unmask myself with you in the hall of love.
I take your strikes with the shield of light
and let them melt to the brightness.
Even when it is hard,
it is worth it.

9. I want

I want to rip the mask off your face
and kiss your true lips.
Your hair is wild as feathers,
your face so white, trapped by horror.
I want with my hands melt the ice of your heart,
with my love give you
a new direction of life.
The bright stream is running in your heart
making your soul live,
making your heart beat unaffected,
bubbling with love,
radiating light.

10. You have

You have carried
a hundred different masks on your face,
you have taken a thousand arduous journeys.
Let your light shine from your soul,
let the wisdom of your heart guide your path.
You are infinite,
you are mighty,
you are wisdom and light.
You are love!

11. The mystery of your eyes

The winds are whispering your name to me,
I see sparrows rise to fly
and come to me.
The moonlight embroider a resplendent mosaic
on the white snow and there I see your face,
one I love and one I know.
My heart silences to you,
settles and calms
to the mystery of your eyes.

12. You are

You are a bright mountain stream to me
that runs brightly down from the mountains
and cleanses my heart
and opens the warmth.
You are a clear starry night to me
looking down bright from the sky
and silences my soul
and opens the love.

13. Your divine being

Beauty embraces
you with the veil of mystery
that glimmers light
enchanting me to see
your divine being.
Your soul is beautiful,
its light dancing in your eyes
making you in magic.

14. I bow

I bend in front of your beauty,
I draw thousands of hearts in the water,
and the wind brings them to you
even beyond the offing.
I bow to the light of your soul,
I admire your noble heart,
there is a warm glow in your eyes,
and I love you ever more bounteously.

15. The road takes

The road takes to the shore of love,
where I see the waves longing.
The road takes to the offing of dreams,
where stars draw a map lighting the heart.
The road takes to a storm
where I survive embracing the cape of my love
and leaning on the compass of my dream.
The road takes through life,
drawing a line in the water
only stars see it proving it's there.

16. I will find a road to you

I will find a road to you,
I will find a path crossing yours,
I will find my way to a crossroads
where we shall meet.
I will fly with the wild birds,
I will swim with the swarms of fish.
I will run through forests and over land
as a wolf in a pack of wolves.
Wild and free I will travel through oceans and air,
forests and lands unknown to man.
By paws of wolf I will cross the snowy mountains,
by wings of a bird I will fly over the clouds,
like fish I will swim under the waves.
I will fly on a plain,
we will arrive at the same station,
a ship will cross an ocean reaching a harbor
where you shall be.
I will find a path to you,
I will come as a wind whistling a song you know,
I will come as a white foaming wave to the beach
right next to you,
I am a pebble on your path shining a light,
I am a flower on the side of your road
twinkling with dew,
I am a tree soughing a message of wind to you,
I am a bird in the tree of your life,
and I will sing you the most beautiful love song,
I will paint you a beautiful painting
with the colors of your life.

I will find a path to you,
our ways will cross.
Stars twinkle above the ocean,
over the desert carrying a message of hope within,
the mystical moon is shining its inscrutable light,
the golden rays of sun
warm the heart of love.

17. Wedding waltz

We walked on the flower fields of life together,
for you I picked
the colorful bouquet of flowers of life,
you pressed the garland of flowers on my head
more beautiful than anything.
I lead you to love by reaching out my hand,
touching your heart.
You took my hand bending your soul to me.
I looked into your bright eyes, filling with tears,
and the tender but
strong depth of love glows in them.
I dance with you this waltz of love
in my heart the love calm and deep,
in my soul the strong and good light of love.
Our lives combine in love,
our souls and hearts melt
in the glow of common light.

18. The cosmic circle of love

We are in the circle of sacred cosmic love,
love heals,
love protects,
love gives the blessing to an enlightened heart,
it brings out the wisdom of the soul.

19. Harmony

The golden bowl of my heart raises to your lips
and you get to drink the pink liquid.
You are on fire
and burn in the darkness of the night
entwining in the cape of love.
You are in front of me bare, open and real,
very sensitive and vulnerable.
You are a brave knight of love,
ennobled in my heart.
I give you,
a rose from the rose tree of my heart
and I make your aura glow.
A shield of love forms around you
to protect from the poison arrows of life.
You bring me the pure bowl of your heart
filled with magical energy
and the key of you love opens all my locks
to receive you.
I am in front of you open, true and bare,
very sensitive and vulnerable,
I am the brave princess of love
you press on my hair
the silver crown of femininity.
And the veil of mystery is risen from my face
like the breaking dawn behind the mountains
and the wise light of my soul arises
like the sun to enlighten our lives.
The tender sense of your soul rings lightly to us
uniting our world in harmony.

Our souls bend towards each other
like willows over seething water
creating a bridge for love to cross.
The birds of our heart seek each other
cross the nightly sky,
finally reaching the same harbor and ship.

20. Home

In front of you my soul quiets down
my heart abates, calms down.
With you I am home,
outside the roar of the world.
We create the cosmic circle of love,
making nests to each other's heart.
May the highest bless you,
enlighten your path like brightness.

21. A map

The twinkle of stars is a map for me to you,
the road of hope,
I am guided by the compass of the soul
the aura of your heart is strong,
without you my heart is only a half.

22. The moon

When we meet somewhere
the moon is brightest,
it shines upon your face.
As a moonbeam I come to you,
entwining myself to you
and flowing into your heart as a light.

23. Your eyes

In your eyes I see a bright starry sky,
in your soul the twinkle of stars play.
In your eyes shines the brightest moon,
and my night will never be dark again.
In your eyes ripple the rays of sun,
and no one else means the same to me.
The warmth of your heart heat me up,
the light of your soul enlightens my path.

24. Lullaby

Sleep in the golden cradle of the night
travel with me to the grove of love.
I have looked into your eyes all evening,
now we sleep in the silver cradle of the moon.
I cover you with the blanket of stars,
gently fling the down of love upon you.
We travel together to the hall of dreams
and I get to see your precious soul.

25. The altar

On the altar of my heart,
stands your likeness beautiful and noble,
roses on the rim
and next to it the light of my heart.
The crystal stream of my soul
surges towards you,
it cleans all collisions
between us.

26. The knight of love

The brave knight of love,
beats the evilness of the dragon,
I look in the mirror of my beloved eyes,
I find the truth behind the shields.
Your velvet mantle flows
when you carry me on your arms
through crowds.
Your horse races over the steppes,
I hold you tight,
but almost carefully.
Cold and savage village,
in the midst of the houses we hear a roar
through fierce fire.
We wildly dart to escape to the woods,
there your fire
lights up a flame in my heart.

27. The key

You hold the key,
who guards the gate?
Who grants us to pass,
when shall I meet you?
Am I just a rusty lock,
where your key fits?
You are a miracle worker
that unlocks me all over.

28. A diamond cross

A golden diamond cross
carries faith, hope and love.
Blessing of the Lord's touch,
entwines the sacred patronage,
a light radiates
through the connected souls of hearts.

29. The heart

A golden pearl heart is cloaked
by the energy of mystery,
in the dark night the golden path of love runs,
the pure heart opens
to the call of unknown,
carry the golden heart of soulfulness.

30. The birds of longing

The hot crystals of tears burn my heart,
the burning tears of sorrow purify my heart.
I think of you my love,
the birds of longing fly away.
Will the silver quill come to you,
the feather of the mystical bird?
Oh my love, use it to write your name to the book
of my heart,
tell me do you wish to be mine,
walk the bravely
the path until the end of life?
The wolves howl in the forest of pain.
I meet you on the white paths of dreams
and I watch the beautiful twinkle of your eyes,
do I find daring in them
to step in the flow of change,
to surrender to the hands of love?
I surrender to your arms whispering your name
with love.
You reach your hand to me,
in your eyes burn the flames of love.
We are entwined together
and we spin to the crowd of stars.

31. I walk with you

I get to walk with you my love,
I remember your counsel again,
in your eyes flows the light of wisdom,
your soul is full of energy of love,
I think of you with longing always,
in my heart I feel gentleness.
I have walked a long journey with you,
I have kissed your heart so many times,
the strings of my soul ring,
I love living you again and again.

32. The crown

The crown is brightest on the master,
your crown is the most beautiful,
it is the shine of destiny to me.
Your eyes shine like beacons to me
when I need guidance,
you regard protects me on my journeys
and blesses me on my paths.
Your strong and tender heart loves,
my soul longs to be connected with yours,
our souls walk together and
entwine to another.

33. I will come to you

I will once come to you wearied on the path,
I will bring my burden so heavy,
and I am so tired,
you will hold me and comfort gently,
I get to press my head on your shoulder
and see you at last.

34. The touch of destiny

My love from beyond the stars,
I have heard your call once
and I have longed to come to you.
Your eyes so deep and steady shines
beyond the stars,
I wish to share an eternal life with you.
My happiness is bounding in my heart,
you will always me in my core,
our souls are tied together
you are the touch of destiny.

35. Me and you

Me and you,
we have seen and lived through a lot
and now we stand here facing each other.
Many years have passed,
many tears have flown,
the sweat of pain,
the blood of longing.
Why are your eyes so strange,
they do not twinkle anymore?
The world have thrown our emotions,
the storms took the needless away.
Oh, it is all here and now,
forget the past,
leave the future.
All that is behind us
here, today just two meet.
The future is strange, unknown.
Life, destiny takes you,
no one will be safe from it.
Me and you,
here and now,
aeon has passed
and we still have an eternity.

36. Love

Love is to give freedom,
to trust the happiness arriving,
bear the bitterness of life.
Love is to be altruistic,
give even though you would get nothing,
to help,
to serve with the light of your soul.
Love is unconditional,
approves the other one the way he is,
gives help and support in hard times,
a possibility and a new beginning.
Love welcomes with joy,
opens up to the other one's energies,
surrenders unconditionally to the higher call.
Love gives time and space,
lets go and gives up when needed,
working for the other one's good.
Love believes in the best,
wishes for dreams to be fulfilled,
keeps up loyalty.
Love believes in guidance,
eternal connection of souls,
bond of two hearts.
Love is always, everywhere,
a bridge of light glittering in your own soul,
a bowl of energy in your heart.
Love wins all,
it's the greatest power in the universe.

37. The chain of hearts

Love glowing from the heart, delicate,
in the chain of hearts,
the beloved stands out as the most beautiful,
with warmth I remember you,
as light I long to get to you.

38. The mystical night

The mystical eyes of the night staring at you,
demanding you to face yourself,
the light flashes
and the soul flies free to the shadows of the night.
A guide, wise and old,
walking with you in the shape of a wolf,
ravens of the subconscious floating above you.
Forest, without a sound,
standing and guarding your steps,
in the dawn, the shadows of the night fade
into the golden flames of the sun.

39. A message

A wolf stepping out from shadows,
with moon's glow in his fur,
in his eyes, lanterns burning,
of an ancient and wise soul.
A message he brings to you,
arrive to the throne of your light,
take the cloak of love onto your shoulders
and rule your fate with changes.

40. A guide

The moon, with its silver magic,
covering the earth with a bright night.
A silver veil shading my eyes,
from my look, shines the wisdom of the soul.
Enters an old man, with his cloak,
and I start to follow him.
Owl crying somewhere on its branch,
flying with the man, with silent wings.
The light of the moon, spotting the nightly forest,
river of time floating somewhere far away.
I cross the bridge into eternity,
my soul opens a window into something new.

41. Give me roots

The Higher Power, the Great Spirit,
give me roots,
to unite with the core of Earth,
let my roots dig down
to the heart of Mother Earth
and draw its power,
let me feel I belong to my own pack,
in which we howl together to the same moon,
jog together wild, to the same goal,
where support is always near
and everyone has their mission,
where everyone can trust each other.
Let me draw from the bowl of abundance,
let the cornucopia fulfill over and over again.
Let nature always speak to me
and let my inner self always quiet down and listen.

42. Give me wings

My Higher Self,
Give me wings,
to fly into the sky of blue,
let my wings carry over mountains,
over seas, over forests.
Let my wings of wisdom
help to solve problems,
flow of creativity take me
to the beach of my dreams,
carry my wings into freedom,
where my thoughts fly
with wings of an eagle, up and far,
enjoying on open seas,
where my imagination carries me
with its wild wings,
Let my soul guide the flight of my wings,
them being clean and shiny.

43. A mysterious blessing

A mysterious blessing falling on your soul
when you start walking your own path.
Your heart's secret wisdom
leading your way.
An angel walking beside you, guiding,
protecting your dream with its wings.
Follow your dream into the dark unknown,
so the light of your soul can shine.
Life answers you with its love
when you surrender to serve the world.

44. Archangel Michael

The blue cloak protects you,
heavenly Michael guards you.
Step boldly into the raging stream of time,
face the changes, surrendering.
Accept your life mission
and cut the outdated bonds.
Sword of Light will cleanse the past,
renew your aura with light.
You are safe wherever you go
when Michael is by your side.
Your Guardian Angel
receives its mission from him
Ask for help and you will get it
when you share your joy to the world.

45. A wolf

A wolf, with silver fur, howling its longing,
the moon's silver coin shining
on the dark velvet of the night sky.
Stars glittering like icy diamonds,
in wolf's eyes, crystals of tears.
From the pack, a wolf left ages ago
to follow its own path,
just longing for a soulmate
to jog together with.
The wolf is guiding souls into the right path,
Northern Lights are just a sign to your own mind.
Lonely footprints remain in the snow,
the wolf leaves its blessings behind.

46. Dogs

Tame dogs walk in packs
always looking for company,
they cannot be alone
and do not enjoy being on their own.
Wild dogs wander alone their own paths,
they cannot live in a pack,
and do not really need company.
Tame and wild dogs hardly ever meet,
you can hear the tame dogs' barking from afar
as they keep noise in the pack,
but the path of the wild dogs
leads into unknown forests
as they look for peace and harmony.

47. The eyes of the night

I have the eyes of the night,
they make me dream.
I have the shining eyes of the night,
they make me see behind everything.
I have the light eyes of the night,
They are like bright stars of the sky,
with them I can look down to bothers of the earth.
I have the eyes of the night,
they shine silver like the full moon of wintry sky.
I have the eyes of the night,
sometimes they can scare others.
I have the eyes of the night
and into the night I disappear,
leaving my eyes to light others' way.
I have the eyes of the night,
in darkness I wander with the light of my soul.

48. The raven

The raven flies from the shadows of the land,
and joins my company.
An eye following the wanderer,
a feather drops beside me.
Way of feathers leading me,
I hear the inner voice call.
A mirror reflection from the water,
a soul is reflected from the eye.
Be still in the shadows of the land,
the soul is only wandering in light.

49. The magic forest

A bird flying with silent wings,
as a fairy in the forest of dreams I sneak.
On a water lily I sail to the river,
moving in a delicate way.
With wings of a butterfly I can fly,
as a bluebell in the meadow I ring.
There's white magic in the summer night,
when autumn arrives, darkens the land.

50. I am

I am an alchemist of love,
the key holder of my lover's heart,
I am a miracle worker with soul,
I am a warrior of light, a spiritual messenger.
I am a guide of the spiritual path,
I am a seeker of light,
a carrier of light in the gloomy forest,
I am a lighthouse in the waves of the sea,
I am a lonely wolf under the moonlight,
I walk my own paths under the stars of the sky.

51. An angel

An angel with wings of light sneaks to you,
embraces you,
always walks beside you.
I want to love you,
give you all the good,
from the depths of my heart,
unconditionally from the soul.
You are an important teacher to me,
you are the best of all.
You teach great things,
you are the alchemist of love,
you are the key holder,
you are a miracle worker.
You teach me how to love,
how to trust,
how to believe in miracles.
I am grateful to you,
I am mute in front of your beauty,
you quiet down my restless sea,
calm down my cross sea.

52. Transformation

I am the princess of love,
my cloak is golden purple.
Above my head, shines the light of a devoted,
I have a crystal house.
The touch of my hand is blessing,
your fate is unknown to you.
I look deep into your eyes,
their golden whirls,
how beautifully glows the energy of your soul.
I touch it with love, and your light brightens,
the rulers of darkness all fade away in time.
How the book of your soul opens in front of me,
the flower of love in your heart glows for a moment
and opens up to the light.
We step towards each other
and our hands join palm against palm,
our soul energy is united
and for a moment I can experience
this magic of a foreign faraway land,
the closest and dearest after all.
This transformation makes us change,
it opens many doors in us.
You, alchemist of love, with your key
you open my heart's secret chamber,
the lid of the treasure chest of my soul opens.
You are a miracle worker,
who leads me
into a never ending fairytale.
The roses of love open in us,
the light flowers of soul glow without withering.

53. The alchemist of hearts

The alchemist of hearts,
your heart's wisdom weighs my dreams,
the light of your soul reveals my development.
The energy of your love
recognizes my heart and soul,
you change my heart into gold,
you bring transformation within,
you give a new beginning and chance.
You are a dream to me,
fulfillment of my dreams,
you are the brightest star
in the sky of a darkening night,
you guide me and give me hope.

54. The drop

The alchemist of love
the drop of love
the drop of the ocean
the drop of tears
the drop of blood
the drop of the universe.

55. The silver ring

With the silver ring bewitched
by the Moon Goddess
I engage to you with my feminine energy
to become intact and whole,
in radiation of your masculine sun energy.
Magic of eras embraces us
and my ring seals
our creative process of development towards
the endless open seas of the mystery ocean
of soul love.
In the moment of our encountering
the diamonds of our souls creates
a sparkling rainbow of our connection between us
and our hearts' tunes play
the melody of a new life phase.
The glowing silver of the moon enchants
the warm gold of your eyes with its mystery.
The radiating gold of the sun lightens
the cloudy sky of my eyes with its brightness.

56. The bowl of love

In the bowl, the clear water sparkles,
I can feel your wondrous love.
The water of life flows through me,
it cleansed everything from my heart.
A bright teardrop gives the magic,
from the spirit of love it carries the message.
Trust the bowl of love,
trust the loving hand.
Sacrifice yourself when the heart tells you to,
the page of fate turns,
taking the old into the oblivion.
Accept the power of love,
let your heart give the beat of life.
Be open and give all that you have,
receive the treasure of your love.

57. The alchemist of love

On the beach of the foaming ocean
with you I united in the night.
You, were you just a fairytale of the mystic night?
I looked in your eyes
while the moon shone so bright,
strange words we spoke on the sand,
all this remained hidden
in the depths of a diamond heart.
The color of love became its light
sealing the nightly experience.
And the experienced alchemist of hearts
sealed the connection of the souls
with the drop of his blood.
The diamond was cleansed by tears,
and so pure love remained in our souls forever.
On the beach of the foaming ocean
I walk the sand in moonshine again,
and remember our mutual night
and still that alchemist, with his advice.
Time is an illusion, I know it now,
still the connection exists,
I can feel it.
The tune of souls is tolling forever,
and who loves, can hear it.

58. I promise

You step out of the shadows,
I see your beauty so dark,
I feel my love so familiar and strange.
Your voice caresses me,
it surrounds me all around.
I sneak into the velvet night with you,
of the stars of my soul
I make a necklace of light for you.
In your heart I want to settle,
but you are allowed to take your own road.
I will walk beside you, facing all trials with you,
carrying your curse just like mine.
Love sets us free,
your key fits in my lock
and with my own key I open the door of your cage.
We fly into the heights of the sky,
we dive into the depths of the sea,
we walk through the dark forest
leaning on each other,
trusting our fidelity.
I do not want to own you,
I want to give love to you,
accept your love as a great blessing,
I want to share the paths of life with you,
be beside you and endure all.
Love sets free,
love is the key that fits in the lock.
In the dark shadows I promise to live with you,
wherever you are, is my place too.
Dark shadows give way to the light of love.

59. Galaxies

The alchemist of hearts
makes the roses bloom,
opens the buds of love.
He unites our worlds
and opens our locks.
The light of love brightens all,
it makes the roses glow in hearts.
On the petals of the rose, galaxies circle,
the universe is hidden in a rose.
In the core of the galaxies,
shines the brightest light,
the light of love.

60. Seas of our hearts

From the shadows you step up,
your essence is graceful, irresistible.
You offer light for my heart,
play of light and shadows speaking on your face
and you change form, blazing.
I feel your warmth,
glow of your passion,
and gently I press myself against you.
Storming seas of our hearts against each other
seeking peace from each other.

61. Tenderness

A wave of tenderness comes, covering us,
like stream of roaring waves, using powers of love.
I notice you arriving, from afar,
like a swell, rolling from the sea,
and like soft sand of the beach
I am ready to receive you.

62. The spring of secrets

With you I wanted to travel beyond times,
to the spring of secrets
and together dive into it,
solve the mysteries that keep up life.
Together we will find a key
to the lock of life's chains.
The knots of heart open,
when we find a mutual tune.

63. I whisper your name

I whisper your name
like wind in the wood of eternity,
the buzz echoes across millenniums,
into this day,
into this moment.
I see your face,
I see your eyes and behind them many others.

64. Life, Death and Love

I

Do you or do not you want, asks life,
admit or deny, death comes anyway.
I do, I do, answers love, smiling.

II

Life is a dream,
from which death awakens.
Love is always awake
and understands all.

III

Life and death are connected
by dream and oblivion,
demand of love is everything and forever.

65. The throne of love

You sit on the throne of love,
in your hands, the golden bowl of love.
Towards you I step, staggering,
I have been thirsty for a long time.
My cloak of light is dusty,
to me you offer a drink from the bowl
and the scepter of the greatest love.

66. Drums of love

Drums of love banging, demanding us to dance,
our bodies entangle together
under an autumn tree,
raining autumn colored leaves,
clothing our wild bodies.

67. My flame

You are my flame,
missed in my heart,
I walk towards you,
I am nourished in the light of your soul.

68. Eternity

Eternity is a moment
in journey of time and place carrying the infinity.

69. First sea

A drop contains
the wisdom and power of the first sea.

70. In every

Every beginning includes the ending,
in every birth, awaits the death.

71. Together we are all

The rain of your love rinses me,
your seeds arrive,
little drops of light and magic.
The rhythm of your passion bangs me,
we swing on the waves of pleasure,
far away on the open sea of joy and happiness.
Let me unite your core,
with me you can reach the sky.
Together we are all.

72. Freedom

Freedom.
Alternatives and a choice,
river foaming wild, streaming across the woods.
To do what you want,
without thinking of consequences,
an eagle floating in the wind across the skies.
To wander without destination,
without owning anything.
Freedom.
To be yourself,
genuine and incorruptible,
lookalike and size of your own soul.

73. Passion

You slide inside me, slowly and gently,
you are one with me,
your love touches my depths,
the light of your essence lights up my heart.
I blaze with you,
passion oscillates,
pulsates inside me.
Be with me,
give your everything,
take me.
The sound of pleasure erupts from your moist lips,
I let you swarm over me time after time
like a wave to the sand.
I am like a beach,
solid and accepting,
I grant you freedom to come foaming like the sea,
waving, leave and come back.
You're an irresistible power,
the moisture you left behind, lingering in me,
until you are back inside me,
and we are one,
now and forever.

74. Prisoner of longing

Prisoner of longing.
I look at you and I know,
I'm a prisoner, prisoner of longing.
Wildly calling you like a nightly eagle-owl
in the forest of yesterday.
Now,
the ship leaves the harbor of tears, longing.
I dive underneath the waves to reach you
at the beach of tomorrow.

75. A branch of my heart

A branch of my heart bends towards you,
I want to rest against your shoulder.
The bird of longing is flapping its wings
looking for a branch to rest on,
wind quiets down and the sea calms down.
My heart, still restless, is missing you.

76. Together we walk

I grab your hand
and together we walk over the rocky mountains,
finally arriving to the seashore.
Into the foams of the sea we step side by side,
merging to the moonlight.

77. Over and over again

Over and over again,
your fingers play the strings of my innermost.
I dive into deep waters,
drown under the waves of your love,
sink into the bottom of your tenderness,
into the bottom of your golden heart.
Accept everything
that I give to you from the rose tree of my love,
it all belongs to you.
I will crown you, my love, with a wreath of roses,
I will let the sparrows land on my branches.
I smile, I know, I understand.